PUBLISH **HER**™

VISION
BOARD
BOOK

Inspirational Images and Words for Manifesting Your Vision

VISION BOARD BOOK

500+ Inspirational Images and Words for Manifesting Your Vision

Self-help gurus define manifestation as focusing your thoughts on a desired outcome using practices like mindfulness, meditation and visualization. Success with manifestation starts with setting your intention, believing it will happen, and taking active steps toward making your ideas and goals a reality.

A vision board—typically a poster with a collage of words and images that represent what you want to accomplish—is a powerful tool for visualization and manifestation. It's a tangible representation of your goals that you can look at every day. Many people create a vision board as they embark upon a new year, but it's a great motivator any time you want to reach a goal. This book helps make the process of creating a vision board simple and fun.

How to Use This Book

The "Publish Her Vision Board Book" was designed to be cut apart to create your custom vision board. Filled with hundreds of high-quality images and words, the pages were thoughtfully laid out so those with a grid of images are backed by solid-colored or wallpaper pages. That means you can cut out an image without sacrificing an image on the other side.

How to Create Your Vision Board

Engage your creative side and be playful. Don't overthink the process. You could simply flip through the book, cut out the images you love, and create a collage. For a more structured activity, use this process for creating your vision board:

1. **Gather your supplies.** You'll need scissors, plus foam core, tagboard, cardboard or heavy paper for the board, as well as glue or tape to fasten the media to it. You could also pin the images to a tackboard. Consider any personal items you have on hand and may want to include on your board, such as photos and print materials like cards, letters, stickers, etc.
2. **Identify your goals.** Take some time to clarify what's important to you. What are your specific goals for the next several months or year? It may be helpful to narrow it down to a couple of goals for your vision board. You could also focus on one larger goal and the benchmarks for reaching it.

3. **Look for themes.** Are your goals personal or professional or both? Consider how they connect and make a list of specific words and images that represent your intentions, goals and benchmarks. Focus on those that give you the most energy.

4. **Select elements that fit the themes.** Flip through the pages of this book for images and words that align with your vision and get to work slicing and dicing the elements that will adorn your board. Cut around the entire square or just the featured object—whatever fits your vision. Add your personal photos and print materials as well.

5. **Lay out your board.** First do a dry layout of all your media on the board. When it looks right, start gluing, taping or pinning everything in place. Continue layering items until it feels complete.

6. **Display it for yourself.** Once you've finished your board, be sure to post it somewhere you will see it often. Remember, it is intended to be a visual representation of your goals that you can look at every day.

7. **Share it with others.** Displaying your vision board so friends and family can see it can be a great way to hold yourself accountable. It may also inspire others to create a vision board to manifest their goals. We'd love to see it as well! Post a photo or video on Instagram and tag @publishherpress.

We hope you enjoy this book and the process of creating your vision board!

About Publish Her

We believe books make lives better.

Publish Her is a female founded independent publisher dedicated to educating authors and elevating the words, writing and stories of women. We aim to make publishing an attainable, exciting and collaborative process for all.

Many women face obstacles in publishing today. Even more so if she is a woman of color, a woman with a disability, a member of the LGBTQ+ community or any combination of these. Publish Her is on a mission to disrupt the status quo and remove barriers for underrepresented authors. We do so, in part, by providing access to publishing services and programs through grants. Learn more at www.publishherpress.com.

FOLLOW YOUR PASSION

Keep moving forward

PURSUE THE THINGS YOU LOVE DOING.

MAYA ANGELOU

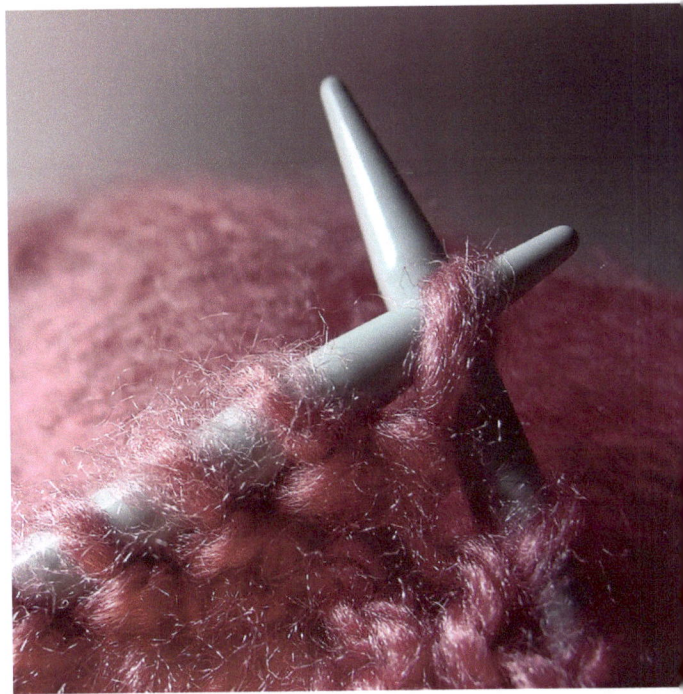

CURIOSITY MUST BE KEPT ALIVE.

ELEANOR ROOSEVELT

SOME LEADERS ARE BORN WOMEN.

GERALDINE FERRARO

Ask for what you want

YOU CAN HAVE IT ALL. JUST NOT ALL AT ONCE.

OPRAH WINFREY

YOUR REPUTATION IS YOUR RESUME.

MADELINE ALBRIGHT

A BIG BUSINESS STARTS SMALL.

RICHARD BRANSON

Dream it, do it

DON'T BE INTIMIDATED BY WHAT YOU DON'T KNOW.

SARA BLAKELY

TRUST YOUR INSTINCTS.

ESTEE LAUDER

LOSE YOURSELF IN THE SERVICE OF OTHERS.

MAHATMA GANDHI

DO THE MOST GOOD

GIVING LIBERATES THE SOUL OF THE GIVER.

MAYA ANGELOU

Listen to your heart

ADOPT THE PACE OF NATURE.

RALPH WALDO EMERSON

Explore new paths

A WALK IN NATURE WALKS THE SOUL BACK HOME.

MARY DAVIS

REST AND RELAX

HELLO, SUN ON MY FACE.

MARY OLIVER

PEACE OF MIND

WE BELONG TO THE EARTH.

CHIEF SEATTLE

Find your happy place

BE A RAINBOW IN SOMEONE ELSE'S CLOUD.

MAYA ANGELOU

It's your time to bloom

A FLOWER BLOSSOMS FOR ITS OWN JOY.

OSCAR WILDE

YOU CAN ALWAYS BEGIN AGAIN

SMELL THE FLOWERS

A day at
the beach is
never lost time

KEEP YOUR FACE TO THE SUNSHINE.

HELEN KELLER

GO TO THE OCEAN

EVERY LEAF SPEAKS BLISS.

EMILY BRONTE

Fall is proof that change is beautiful

sweater weather

AUTUMN IS MORE THE SEASON OF THE SOUL.

FRIEDRICH NIETZSCHE

SNOW FALLS, NATURE LISTENS.

ANTOINETTE VAN KLEEF

GET COZY

WISDOM COMES WITH WINTERS.

OSCAR WILDE

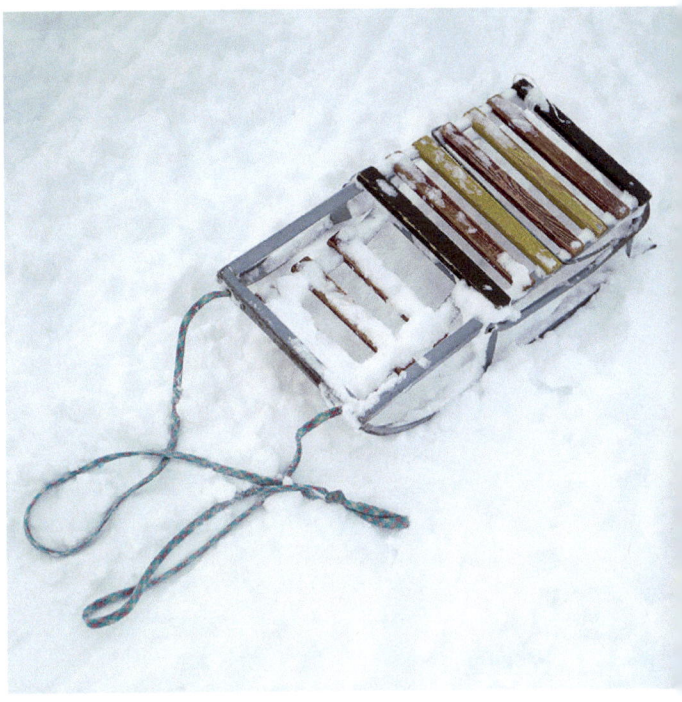

Winter is for wondering

LIFE IS NOTHING WITHOUT FRIENDSHIP.

CICERO

Better together

IT'S SO MUCH MORE FRIENDLY WITH TWO.

WINNIE THE POOH

No road is long with good company

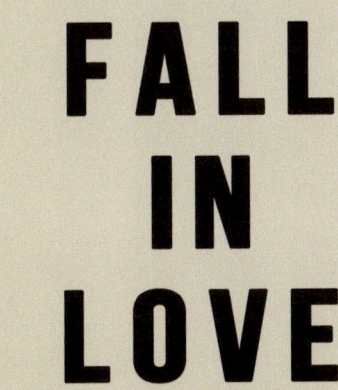

FALL
IN
LOVE

Cherish
moments,
Create
memories

LIFE IS
THE FLOWER
FOR WHICH
LOVE IS
THE HONEY.

VICTOR HUGO

A LOVING
HEART IS
THE TRUEST
WISDOM.

CHARLES DICKENS

SAY
YES

Where there is love, there is life

THE ENTIRE UNIVERSE CONSPIRED TO HELP ME FIND YOU.

PAULO COELHO

TO HAVE AND TO HOLD

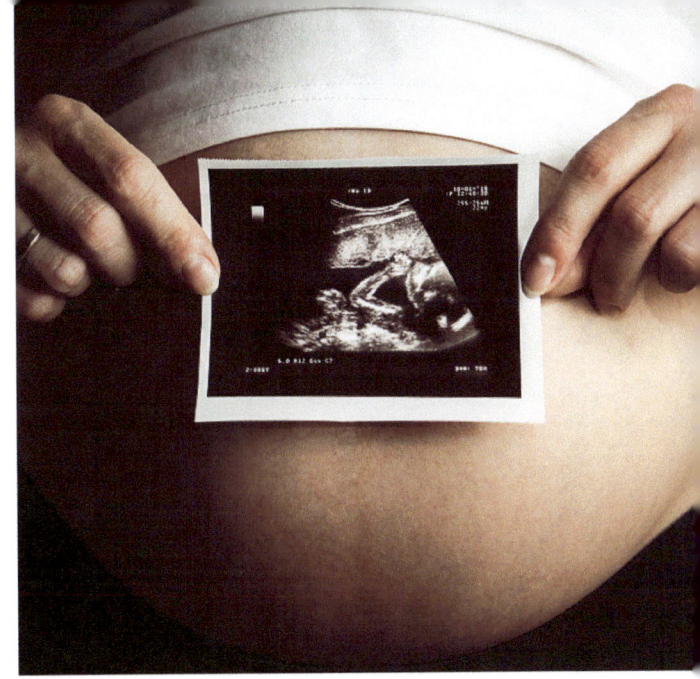

OH,
BABY

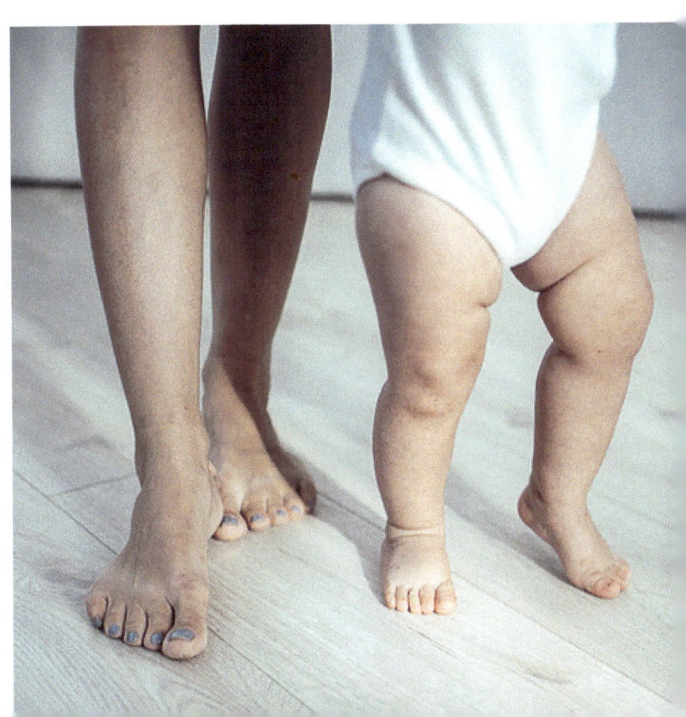

MOTHER IS A VERB

A MOTHER'S ARMS ARE MADE OF TENDERNESS.

VICTOR HUGO

LOVE IS OUR MOTHER.

RUMI

HAPPINESS IS A WARM PUPPY.

CHARLES M. SCHULZ

BE THE PERSON YOUR DOG THINKS YOU ARE.

C.J. FRICK

GOOD DOG

ONE CAT LEADS TO ANOTHER.

ERNEST HEMINGWAY

HOW MANY CATS MAKE A CAT LADY?

TAYLOR SWIFT

Home is where the cat is

BLOOM
WHERE
YOU'RE
PLANTED.

SAINT FRANCIS DE SALES

LOVE GROWS HERE

Plants are better listeners than most people

WE MUST CULTIVATE OUR OWN GARDEN.

VOLTAIRE

PUT YOUR HOUSE IN ORDER.

MARIE KONDO

CLEAR THE CLUTTER

THE LESS YOU HAVE, THE MORE FREE YOU ARE.

MOTHER TERESA

Count memories, not things

THE FIRST WEALTH IS HEALTH.

RALPH WALDO EMERSON

Eat the rainbow

LET FOOD BE THY MEDICINE.

HIPPOCRATES

FARM TO TABLE

COOKING
IS LIKE
LOVE.

HARRIET VAN HORNE

GOOD FOOD

PEOPLE WHO LOVE TO EAT ARE THE BEST PEOPLE.

JULIA CHILD

FOOD IS OUR COMMON GROUND.

JAMES BEARD

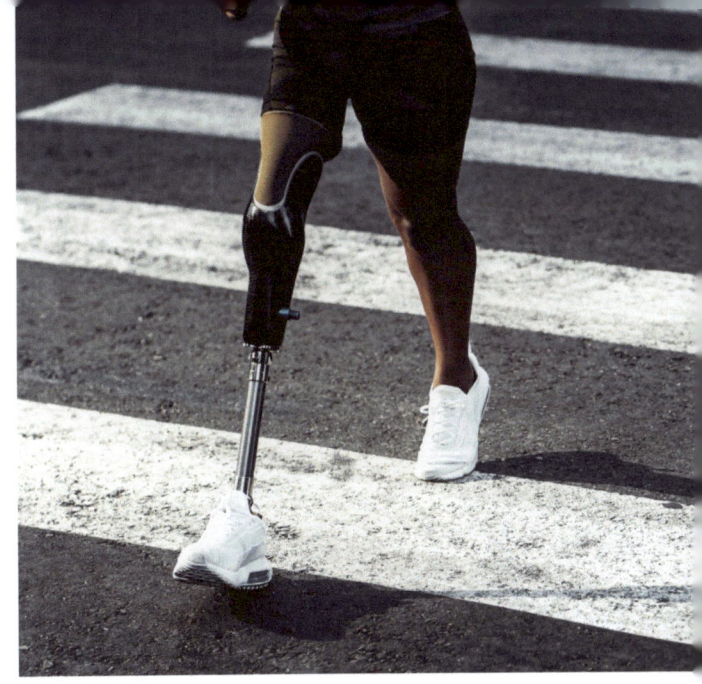

AN EARLY MORNING WALK IS A BLESSING.

HENRY DAVID THOREAU

MOVE YOUR BODY

EVERY HUMAN IS THE AUTHOR OF THEIR OWN HEALTH.

THE BUDDHA

You are more than enough

KEEP TAKING TIME FOR YOURSELF.

LALAH DELIA

LET GO

YOU WON'T BE HAPPY UNTIL YOU LOVE YOURSELF.

LADY GAGA

INSIDE OF US EVERYTHING BLOOMS.

ALICIA KEYS

PRAYER IS NOT ASKING.

MAHATMA GANDHI

LOVE AND LIGHT

Walk the path of enlightenment

LET THE BREATH LEAD THE WAY.

SHARON SALZBERG

WEALTH IS THE ABILITY TO FULLY EXPERIENCE LIFE.

HENRY DAVID THOREAU

KNOW YOUR WORTH

DON'T MAKE MONEY YOUR GOAL.

MAYA ANGELOU

Define your own wealth

THE CITY IS LIKE POETRY.

E.B. WHITE

NEW YORK IS ALWAYS HOPEFUL.

DOROTHY PARKER

EMPIRE STATE OF MIND

The city that never sleeps

LIVE, TRAVEL, ADVENTURE, BLESS.

JACK KEROUAC

SHE'S LIKE A RAINBOW

PEOPLE DON'T TAKE TRIPS, TRIPS TAKE PEOPLE.

JOHN STEINBECK

It is all uphill from here

PARIS IS A MOVEABLE FEAST.

ERNEST HEMINGWAY

OOH, LA LA

WHEREVER YOU GO, GO WITH ALL YOUR HEART.

CONFUCIUS

Bonjour, mon ami

LONDON CALLING

JUST CLOSE YOUR EYES AND THINK OF ENGLAND.

QUEEN VICTORIA

NOT ALL THOSE WHO WANDER ARE LOST.

J.R.R. TOLKIEN

A rising tide lifts all boats

FEELING SAUCY

Adventure awaits

CIAO, BELLA

IN WINE THERE IS TRUTH.

ITALIAN PROVERB

DO NOT SQUANDER GOLD LIKE EARTH.

CHINESE PROVERB

OH, THE PLACES YOU'LL GO.

DR. SEUSS

EVERYTHING HAS BEAUTY, BUT NOT EVERYONE SEES IT.

CONFUCIUS

Life is short and the world is wide

PEACE COMES FROM WITHIN.

THE BUDDHA

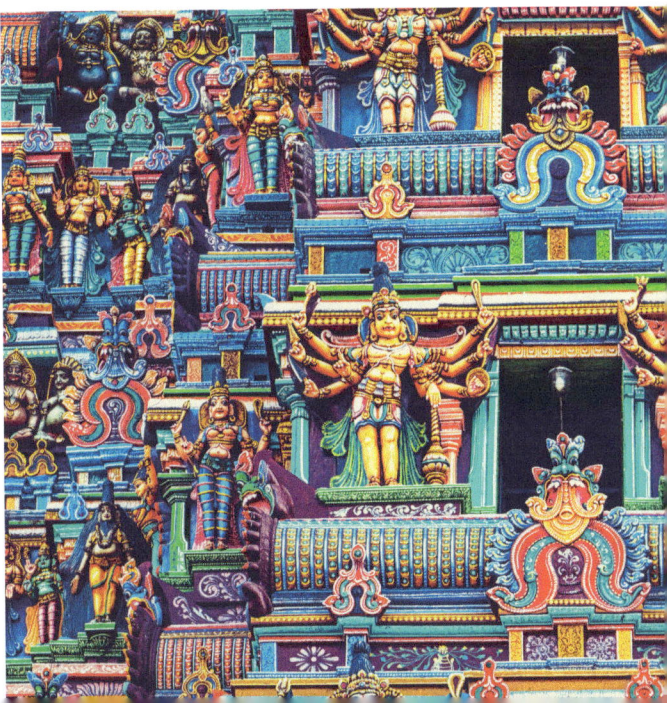

TRUTH ALWAYS WINS

FALL IN LOVE WITH YOUR SOLITUDE.

RUPI KAUR

GOOD KARMA

THE RIVER FLOWS NOT PAST, BUT THROUGH US.

JOHN MUIR

The mountains are calling

CHOCOLATE IS MY LOVE LANGUAGE

TRAVEL WITH NO REGRET.

OSCAR WILDE

WE MUST BUILD AS IF THE SAND WERE STONE.

JORGE LUIS BORGES

The journey begins

A BEAUTIFUL THING IS NEVER PERFECT.

EGYPTIAN PROVERB

PAST PRESENT FUTURE

NO
WORRIES

TRAVELER, THERE IS NO ROAD.

ANTONIO MACHADO

YOU'RE DOING AMAZING, MAMA

ROAM IF YOU WANT TO

Don't wait for opportunity, create it.

STEP OUTSIDE YOUR COMFORT ZONE

BETTER LATE THAN NEVER

Today is a new beginning

Make your own magic

DREAM BIG

BE YOU

Never give up

Being a woman is a superpower

TRUST THE PROCESS

YES YOU CAN

Nevertheless, she persisted

Start somewhere

HELL YEAH

TRAVEL

Reality check

Dreams have no expiration date.

SMALL BUSINESS OWNER

WE RISE BY LIFTING OTHERS

Grateful for this moment

Manifest that shit

START FRESH

HAPPY

Be here now

GOOD
THINGS
ARE
COMING

MAKE
IT
HAPPEN

YOU
GOT
THIS

You only
live once

Word of
the year

DEBT
FREE

GROW

Love yourself

The path you take is entirely up to you.

YOU HAVE THE POWER TO CHANGE YOUR LIFE

Happily ever after

BORN LEADER

Stronger every day

DARE

CEO

Keep going

COURAGE	WORTHY
Intention	BALANCE
GRATEFUL	Transform
PROGRESS	IMPROVE
ORGANIZE	VISION
LEARN	PLAY

ABCDEFGHIJKLMN
OPQRSTUVWXYZ
0123456789

ABCDEFGHIJKLMN
OPQRSTUVWXYZ
0123456789

ABCDEFGHIJKLMN
OPQRSTUVWXYZ
0123456789

ABCDEFGHIJKLMN
OPQRSTUVWXYZ
0123456789

ABCDEFGHIJKLMN
OPQRSTUVWXYZ
0123456789

ABCDEFGHIJKLMN
OPQRSTUVWXYZ
0123456789

ABCDEFGHIJKLMN
OPQRSTUVWXYZ
0123456789

ABCDEFGHIJKLMN
OPQRSTUVWXYZ
0123456789

ABCDEFGHIJKLMN
OPQRSTUVWXYZ
0123456789

PUBLISH HER™